SHE GOES TO TOWN

Sandra Renew

SHE GOES TO TOWN

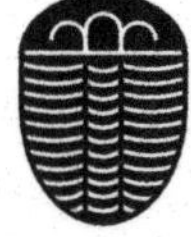

PART I

Part 1: I Am Writing from the Body of Who I Am Now …

She separates herself. There are different voices here, and separations. Cutting away

from her past, from varied, acceptable and permissible futures dreamed into expectations by others on her behalf. From always being a dangerous difference in a country town, and rural school. Segue to wide-eyed in the city, to wild eyed, in a city never imagined.

There will be reversals. Finding again broken and unreliable links, going back. Travelling old roads as if she only knew them in dreams.

Two voices, more than that. Speaking her uncertain, new urban body, new words … a separation. From all the ones she becomes, from the country and landscape and rural town which sent her on her way. She is writing a memoir, a fiction of herself, reminiscing remembrances, maybe an obituary …

Street

she owns the street, she is the street,
and the street is desire and lust, a sideways welcome
for all the wrong reasons and
a spit on the tarmac for being unreachable

when she looks through the heat haze shimmer
she sees the line of folded mountain
she sees her body lying prone, at ease
along a horizon that is more than away

she traces the line of blue on blue
with her outstretched fingertip
she never lies with so much quiet
eyes closed, eons of dreaming, never that

she is that road stretching from the last servo
waiting for heat haze dazzle to settle
through country amazed by tiny lizards and wild dogs
to the unwinnable mountains

when she walks from her truck
to the street, to the pub, all eyes see her
men want her, her easy stride in heavy work boots
wind grit muscling in under her dried-out oilskin

men know she's off limits, not a woman for them
women's eyes squint as their mouths narrow
and shopping day lipstick bleeds in cracks and furrows
they hope their men know her for what she is …

when she looks around everyone knows
she is looking, what she does to the street
says Fuck you! When she looks at you and nods
she says I see you. And now, she is the street

I have seen her seeing some women
some women who walk like her
who heat space like a cool burn
those few women who lie on the horizon like her

folded, prone, distant, whose hands reach for her
who light wildfire for each other
whose sunburnt skin is moving dune
and love, like tiny tracks, skitters and flirts

Woman Cross-dressed, Cross-pressed

sartorial elegance is often in fashion
when cross dressing spectacle
is role transgression

masks at festival make masquerade
an entirely foreseeable inevitability
for drag dressed women

across the room some looks askance
but lingering on a second glance
poise and confident self-possession

cross dressed androgyny
for situations of mutual attraction
there's no confusion

love at first sight, ask no questions
mischievous joy in gender allusion
variation in gender is no digression

if aim to question social presumptions
of male and female dualism
cross dressing allows a decompression

Once We had a Revolution

when someone in evil calls her a homo and a dyke
she *knows* she's her history, her rage is deep from here—
she rages from here, from her blood and body

when it seems that all that revolution has not merited
one footnote, all that revolution turned us
from 'a little bit dykey' to a strut, a swagger, a sashay, a suit …

she won't let it pass without comment
the 'put down', the crush, the quash, the quell
she's far from June Dally Watkins country

and Manuka's fashion street is not top of mind—
when she riffs her rage on fancy fashion frocks
the room goes quiet

social media sucks in its collective breath
her time of rage in history makes her a footnote
but with all that revolution she is not just a footnote

now she is the whole of history—I have seen her once, silenced
by power and evil, but now she *is* her history, her history *is* her story
she knows the banality of evil, of how you are co-opted to hate us

how the words become the lie
how the lie becomes the story
how the story becomes the history
how the history becomes the narrative
how the narrative becomes the discourse
how the discourse becomes *her body*

in the small things, the spit, the slagging off, the casual assault
she must be the revolution
she always has to accept the hatred of the journey

to *wait* for journey's end, to wait for coming home.

She Goes to War

she falls off the moon, prisoner of her life
no wings to spread in time, this time, or yet
what's done in darkness or even with a shadowed moon

either by her or to her can never be finally
hidden or forgotten or lost
impersonating is incitement

the court of everyone is shocked and scandalised when she appears
her hair short, rough-cut with pinking shears
and wearing men's clothes

the sentence is demolition, she is the demonstration
between covers they've made her with words no-one should use
written and said by a gown and wig with lurid intent

turned on its head it all becomes her violence
a dyke on attack, and who has a right to offend
is the question, the implication is

implicating the moon in her madness …
if there are horses on the moon feed them
thunder and fire, the smell of war

Take a Moment

Search for green cool, snapshots of summer: river swims, stream tennis or cricket, search for RATs, coming soon to a chemist near you. Radio news, as a breath of safe air brings an entertaining farce of politics—on the face of it a La Niña summer could be worse.

Check out an everyday sunrise, inevitability of a new sky—taste fresh bread, smell brewed coffee, an anthem of detail still in evidence for daily tests during viral freedom. Air kisses still kisses, shadow kisses, even beamed at zoom length, backgrounded by SummerNats' rev and rumble, engine echo rebound.

Lined up on the kitchen window ledge, pretending to be oranges, masquerading as sweet, delicious, smooth skinned citrus delight. And we bought a bag of them at a roadside stall, lugged them to the back seat of the dripping Volkswagen, then into the kitchen bench. But they are the rejects, tart, mouth-shudderingly sour. We wonder what fair usage would be, to avoid dumping them as waste, given the trick they played to seduce us into purchase, their bitter, inner truth costumed in soft, sun-glowed skin.

In a La Niña summer, a day when rain eases at noon, ducks feed on grass-drunk snails, caution abandoned on street edge. Frogs that called through a humid dawn sing harmony into day, sing on into afternoon, a new lease of life at dusk. From deep under earth they have come, from burrows under drought dried soil, crevices dug down to stay with damp. In full throated roar they give voice, sing joy, share rhythm, harmony, timing their parts to perfection. They're not dancing, it's song. Our hill drains to standing water ponds, all low-lying hollows, wheel tracks, reed beds, garden verge. Still they sing.

We look back at ourselves—dinosaurs who created a heat apocalypse, destroying our own planet. In tropical damp, singing over water, we say hello in frog song, an Esperanto—voice of a newly born, post-human planet.

In 2050, a child asks: what was bigger, a viral pandemic or polar bears starving on melting Arctic ice?

She Enjoys Being Older

She enjoys being older, relishes altered perceptions, swigging mouthfuls of freedoms extended to a woman her age. Taking that one step too far, drawing too close to an edge unforgiving, sometimes turning nasty, and taking a little longer to mellow, to come back to the table.

Coming back from the edge, she takes her freedom where she finds it.

Having a decent regard for things
she's the archer freezing time,
aiming for a target,
loosing an arrow.
And then it is too late!
That arrow can never be returned to the bow.
The curse of wanting a perfect score,
an elegant solution,
not marks but words on paper.
An archer can never erase what is written
after a target is struck,
after words are read.
Especially when the substance is open to question,
or not as beautiful or elegant
as one would wish.
So, what will steady her nerves? Still her hands? Focus her gaze?

A door opens and the smell of rain from a cold rose garden rushes through dry air, shouldering aside smells of last week's bodies. Surfaces and spaces invite sensitive fingertips, draw the whole palm and both hands to travel and spread over unseen surfaces, rough plaster, cold door fittings, sharp, sliding under her hand with a frisson of wariness.

Trivialities crowd her mind, unbidden, unwelcome, jostling for space when she would rather think important, critical, useful and perceptive commentary on contemporary and world saving (or at least world changing) discourses.

What to do about these legs of mine which do not seem to me to be as good as I would wish.

Be neither too small nor too big.
Seek true greatness in the richness of your philosophies, thoughts of your citizen neighbours. Sigh ...

Overrun ... with Flow

In threes, nebulae of electrons, like a cloud of dust in deep space, cluster fizzing, insects drawn to a stuttering streetlight, data site, data scraping. Incessant movement. Nothing stops.

i.

Of all shortages we hear about in the city, road-train drivers aren't one. All along motorways, highways and B roads, country corrugations, huge B-doubles hurtle, driverless, liberated, relying for seamless navigation on their own internally resourced GPS, sweet voiced 'Australian Karen', and CB radio tuned to their own mateship network.

Drivers sit and sit. Hopped up, but sitting. Yawning but wide awake. Supply chain depends on seamless flow, on-demand command and both are curves, with on-flow and movement … otherwise, otherwards it's back-up, backed up, stopped up.

ii.

It's been a pretty ordinary sort of year so far (that is, a year in the not-so-good range), most people would probably agree. So, when neurochemical, oxytocin, over-runs her brain, she suddenly finds an unfamiliar urge to social bonding, the whole world population is her family, clan, a racial kinship, and not merely common DNA originating in the Garden of Eden. She feels a pithy over-wroughtness of religious aphorism—*generosity is the antidote to greed, giving is better than receiving, do unto others* etc—of no discernible benefit to the wronged or starved.

On a scale commensurate with her Aunt's admonition that *'diamonds are a girl's best friend'*, she feels selflessly magnanimous, but bereft at lacking her own personal benefactor in either a government pension or invitation to a philanthropic soirée to raise funds for hydroxychloroquine and personal protective equipment.

Holding out her hands, empty, palms up in peace, giving all the skin she has, she realises that a largesse of forgiveness and generalised kindness is not enough. Without the tempered steel of rage and dissent, no-one will move over to make room for her. And she will need more than a chemical brain-flood of oxytocin to move over for anyone else.

iii.

Arthritic pain, it welds her hips,
graph of ageing, pain checkpoint,
one year ago, she still could skip.
Arthritic pain, it welds her hips,
so, hands on hips she comes to grips
with invasive replacement of her joints,
arthritic pain, it welds her hips,
graph of ageing, pain checkpoint.

Keep moving even if it feels like bone grinding on bone, making you weep, with gritted teeth, with pain and self-pity: *Movement will cause a flushing of the synovial joint with synovial fluid*—an egg-white, joint oiling, desperate hope for elasticity …

No miracle sinecure, as synovial
fluid floods her joints,
nothing remedial or magical when pain is so custodial.
No miracle sinecure, as synovial
fluid, hard at work, attempts to be stoical.
Flexibility reduced to vanishing point,
no miracle sinecure, as synovial
fluid floods her joints.

iv.

Many things can be true at once. Possibilities for a good worry flow through her mind. She worries about the geopolitical changes in world power structures at the same time as the plumber unblocks the kitchen sink, frowns at the ancient metal pipes, sends the apprentice into spider world under the deck. Should she worry first about the apprentice and the spiders? Knowing that Australia may be nuked to serve as a lesson to the big powers. The only likely winners will be arachnophobia-inducing nightmares, the spiders, who will not only survive but thrive in a non-human future. Or should her focus be on the world powers with nuclear weapons? On failures in the supply chain? On pain management reduced to drug dependence? Or is it expanded?

v.

smoke caught in sunlight
dirt road dips into a dark rain-forest gully

On the radio news: *his truck*
a weapon driven into peaceful
protesters
women, children, scream, run
would crushed bodies make his point?

on Melting Ice and Research on the Penis

people like us, silenced, have many unsung words:
restraint, recycle, renewable, habitat, science, forewarning—
and here am I giving them up as gifts, in reciprocity,
to claim my respect for a planet alive since the beginning of time—
ice melt, portent, canary, ambiguous, onset, overdue

—

an idea of balance, although, here and now we are crazy ants—
canary is the kick-pleat keystone allowing us to change our minds
mainsprings of yesterday's news, a Necker-cube of ambiguous perspective
things that happen between cracks, portents and onsets,
worthy openers to tomorrow, to what happens yesterday

—

for a woman going out, a woman and a woman
coffee in an autumn with a dog
good news research is now imminent and prolific on long-covid, since
covid's humour in keeping the penis deflated is today's disaster,
opening scientific investigation avenues un-imagined until risk to the masculine
becomes the ice melt, portent, keystone more critical than
a planetary demise of living life due to global warming warnings ...

Back Story of a Country Girl

It was *West Side Story*, Sharks vs the Jets, Protestants vs Catholics, Meredith, 1961. An uneasy, snarky, gossipy small-town melee of enforced separations. The twelve-seater school bus, bringing farm kids from the Soldier Settlements, passed by St Joseph's Catholic school, stronghold of the town kids. *Cathos* we shouted out the bus windows, *Proddies*, they yelled back. This was as far as it went until St Joseph's closed temporarily, being unable to attract a teacher.

One Monday, there they were, on our turf, scuffing their shoes on our playground asphalt, as our teacher introduced them as our visitors, and enjoined us to treat them kindly. Little-lunch break we circled each other. They were small town kids who owned the town. Their knuckles raw, their voices high and their words rough. Their noses ran yellow and green snot. Their jumpers were thin, frayed and grey at the elbows and cuffs. Their pants and coats were cut down from adult cast-offs. One of the girls, stand-out taller than the rest of us, one stone in her fist ready, pockets already weighed down with a second and third, stood aside, separate. Alert, vigilant. Not really one of them, and definitely not one of us.

Lunch break, *Cathos/Proddies* sledging, then some half-hearted scuffles with two of the bigger boys. There was no Romeo and Juliet, no full-blooded gang war, no casualties. Just an occupying of partisan ground, each group by weight of numbers, taking possession of shelter-sheds, veranda over-hang, grass around the basket-ball court. By home-time, the come-latelies all faded off into town, we got on the bus as usual, the only noticeable difference being the silence in St Joseph's playground as we drove past.

In no time at all it is 1972. The Green Dragon Lounge, George Hotel, St Kilda. She is still the country girl from Meredith, wanting a bigger life (unspecified) before she gets old. And the ancient guy, viewed hazily through the stale cigarette smoke, who claims to be the manager, gives her a job.

Public bar with carpet stink, dull roar of after-work blokes insistent on loading up before they broach the home fires. And TITS (This Is The Show) in neon, a dubious, all-above-board invitation to the worldly—no surreptitious flashers, no overcoats unbuttoned for nefarious purposes, no-one who could be undone. She lasts one trial week behind the bar, *girlie, get a move on, ya need to crack a smile every so often*, even though no visible tits are required, no sign of Vanessa the Undresser during day shifts.

Then, second chance, she's the Bottle Shop cashier behind a scratched, smeared plexi-glass shield, where no-one cares if her hair is too short, no-one comments on her Blundstone boots, or her lack of social repartee. At shift's end, as she is sliding out from behind the cubicle cash register, the hubbub from the bar crowd swells and bursts out into the blue suburban night haze of Melbourne summer. Fame, larger than life, in a voluminous caftan-like shawl brushes past, is briefly outlined in the lighted pub doorway and vanishes inside. Vanessa the Undresser! so close …

Getting 'the Electric'

I thought she would be happy when I put on the 'electric'. A reading light at night for my homework from the Office.

But then, abandon the kero fridge for a plug-in ice box. A machine to wash clothes, throwing out the copper and mangle. She wants a water-heater tank, water boiler, plug-in oven, toaster. A machine for sewing. Switch on lights in the kitchen … and her own reading lamp!

I wasn't ready for it. Her demand for appliances. Managing the Grid is more than science. It's power politics in the raw with secret control centres, interconnected power networks. It's electromechanical generators driven by heat engines, fuelled by combustion or nuclear fission. And now, kinetics with flowing water and wind, photovoltaics, geothermal. Billing gone mad with choice, corseted by the past. She is dazzled by modernisation, and the possibility of invention. But it costs us, no free lunch in this story.

From the generation of the energetic electron, and the amps, watts and volts, to when she presses the wall switch for her daily chores, in that fraction of a milli-second, while the electrics surge through the Grid and down the wire, our Earth heats just a fraction more.

Power politics of home: modem, laptop, I-pad, I-phone, TV, sound system, coffee maker, headphones, micro-wave, radio, heaters, coolers, power tools, vacuum cleaner. All plugged in. And now, she doesn't need her own lamp for reading. All her screens are back-lit.

Use Value: Shaped to Conform

Three million people start with a blank grid, thirty squares, six lines of five. In twenty minutes (averaged out over three years with some pretty shonky data) they all pump the air in victory. Send a share message to all their friends with appropriate emoji comment.

Their brains are all being shaped to conformity every time they do this daily exercise.

The Tesla EV provides a vehicle for the rapture. Luxurious, taking off in privileged salvation, only those in the club share the secret smugness of knowing the locations of the private Tesla charging stations. Luxuriate in the heated, shape shifting seat. Press the brake pedal. Your rapture chariot powers on and is ready to drive. If you have sudden second thoughts about driving into the sky press *Park* and exit the vehicle. It will power off by itself, its screens will darken. The car will be suddenly rendered a road not taken. And if a robot at a central control station, for example, the one that picks the Wordle word each day, suddenly develops autonomy, or a self-starter appears, and presses the brake over-ride, all Tesla drivers could suddenly be overtaken by the rapture and be risen up, ready or not.

The use value of Wordle and of the EV is in the fact that for one we have no tangible use. For the other, our survival depends on it. We need the learned conformity of one to push ourselves into the other. What else but obedience and conformity will make us shrug off the petrol, fossil fuelled known and take a seat in electrics, swap the known for the unknown, over-ride our fear? And why has it taken us so long?

Where is the anger in this story? All through it, is the answer. Like marbled beef (an appalling desecration and abuse of our kindred co-inhabitants of the planet, by the way). We are every which way, all over the place. Occasionally. Every so often. When the anger is greater than the fear, we want to know what you are so afraid of.

PART 2

This is Where I Come From, What I Came Through to Get Here

As long as she can remember there was a search for a way to come in from the outside. The family, a spinning centrifuge, sucking some members deeper into significance, spinning and spinning, flinging her out, off the edge, a road corner with poor camber, nothing to nudge her back to the centre.

Connection becomes a separation from both culpability and regret. Memory is a memoir of what we are losing. Telling memory as story becomes an anthem of both sorrow and hope. There is always a sense of returning …

Tribe

There are at least four hundred and forty-seven usages of the word *cry* in the English language. And we are using all of them in our stories of conversations, histories of wars among ourselves and iconic acts of resistance. I don't think I am being romantic when I look around me and cannot find my tribe, either in the past or any present. Neither is it visible to me in futures we once saw ahead of us, and which are now, through our own hands, not.

I have no wistful affection for what we have seen in my generation. Songs changed from year to year instead of ballads and sagas standing as history from century to century. Humanity, without understanding our dependence on the life of earth, crying for the moon, creating an endless noise of conflict. Not understanding that if you are wealthy and white, what the Other has is not to be coveted. Keening in anguish when it is our turn to pack up a very small number of items that we own and begin to walk away, long lines of exodus reflecting parables of past lessons.

Screaming, wailing for all we have insisted on, that we thought essential to happiness. Even as oceans engulf us, and salt permeates everything we know and own and do. When all creation that we care about ends, it is too late. When trees send help and warnings to each other we cannot believe it.

We have an invidious ability to destroy. We blur moral edges when we cannot see what deserves to be named as war, too distant, not personal. It happened when it happened, that summer when La Niña poured down rain like an elixir to heal scars of fire, settle smoke, ash, dust from seven years of drought and a planetary catastrophe of fire. That summer when rain rediscovered runnels and rills the land had made and forgotten. That summer, expectations of heat and light and sun never happened. Trees dropped leaves in a premature autumn before we were ready.

As we left the house that morning we had no idea that when next we opened the door, our world as we know it, would have changed forever. Between us we had a thermos of coffee, three cans of suffragette purple and green spray paint, black for the graffiti, and ready for a banner, two broom handles (never used) and a folded sheet. She had her smart watch, billed as *wireless-enabled wearable technology,* although I could never see the attraction of being monitored 24/7 myself, and I had the door key.

Immediately we were in the street and sucked into the crowd, all bodies flowing purposefully towards the centre of power, a druid hollowing out of a hill, pretending to be of the people but a hot bed of malfeasance and misogyny and homophobia and … . All purporting to be of our tribe, outraged by the same things, costumed in the same acceptability. But all at once, obviously, not of the same mind. We were suddenly unsure, again, if we were the agents of our actions or the targets of others, outsiders, perennial gender refugees. Enduring wariness and caution, forever divided from the centre by boundaries of difference.

It all started with a strong desire to wear trousers, to be more than they were allowed to be. This was Coco Chanel and Marlene Dietrich in the 1920s, and David Bowie being Ziggy Stardust, and Annie Lennox cutting off her hair.

All for the no regrets performance of androgyny. Gender fluid, gender queer. The look that the parents and aunts and teachers all named 'selfish', implying as it did, in those times before turkey basters, the 'no grandchildren' sense of loss, righteous indignation that the generations would break. 'No use crying over spilt milk' approach of the pragmatic.

It happened as we were counselled to look outwards, not inwards, as a protection against depression, anxiety and too much 'bookishness', eventual suicide, destruction of the family. We found the *umwelt*, the world as it is experienced by us. In our *umwelt*, turning the tables, engaging with the world immediately around us, we made it our own self-centred world. A world of Mardi Gras, gay and lesbian night clubs and bars, a world known only to us as we discovered people like us, when we had thought we were the only one, engaged with a community of gender queer. Lovers, ex-lovers, more ex-lovers, co-parents.

So once the trousers and make-up translated across the binary we were off and running, home and hosed, so to speak, and androgyny rules.

Gender climate reasserts itself. The old antagonisms, fears for the nuclear family, rejection of difference, break through the surface veneer of tolerance like molten lava in all the gay hate crimes perpetuated by cowards out of sight and out of reach of legal justice. Cries of bigots, moralists, and homophobes cut deep, cut fatally. The *umwelt* is not benign for those of us who are of the alphabet. A crying out in the wilderness of the *umwelt*. It is important to know how much we are hated.

Just Goes to Show

her city clothes are all the go
dressed up to the nines, her father says,
all set to make a go of it
in a way we couldn't—

just have a go, says her brother, give it your best shot, give it a go—

but they mean get a good job,
she means get a new life
she's going to town to do the town

out the front door, backpack slung over one shoulder
bus stop in the distance, out past the cemetery
she walks past all the dying flowers

just goes to show, you can do it if you do it

is her body leaving? Is her mind gone?
she's dressed to kill with dreams and discontent

they eye her off from inside the servo, but she's making herself scarce,
not doing it by halves
she gets on the bus
through the wheezing automatic door, and up the steep steps
hands in her ticket

making her way in the new hot city, she checks
what currency she has or is
things are looking up, until, computer down—bring money
her new clothes are old clothes, recycled for carbon points,
fashion resale, preloved and abandoned
the city is feeding itself around her,
and the sea is powering spangled lights
rising hig h er as it warms, swamping, tearing,
ripping, tidal, super tides now the norm
we're all made of stardust, it depends how you look at it
neon doomsday sign offs and count downs
all our exuberant futures, on hands-free auto pilot

Nose Drip

It is a day, just a nose drip away from summer,
a day that is a bit of all right, really
a day we muster a thousand head of drought-master cattle
from the free-range desert country pasture to stockyards and
bush camp
sitting around in firelight with tea and rum
and then she kills a man …

she kills his ego, punctures his pride
deflates his bombast, points to his gut,
compares him negatively to an AFL footballer,
talks back to his mansplaining
laughs at his penis, specifically the size of it
gestures to his genitals with a sharp leather-flailing knife …

she knows the moment
she goes off him
knows she will go through with it
the getting out from under
nothing she will miss or go without—
definitely the day for it

End Scene

I saw her the first night. She came on the scene like a wisp of smoke. Ephemeral. Adding to the comings and goings, pairings and couplings, breakings and partings, all the scene we've come to expect. Necessary if there's a flame, but smoke in your eyes is not helpful for clarity.

Elusive. She seemed to exist in the upbeats, any space between notes she was there, but on the downbeats, whole building pulsing, trembling with staccato drum beat, she faded back, elbowed out. Not much room for a shy shimmy when women are dancing. Pounding drums, stamping feet, boots and bare soles, jeans and ethnic skirts, braids and shaved heads. Sweat, incense, a sharp underline of rum, or scotch. Dust stamped from the floorboards, shaken from the walls, ceiling rocking.

Most nights, for the festival week, we hooked up. No need for conversation, just the body work. But, and it's a big one, no chance of a conversation. Just to underline intentions. Make a plan. Concept of future. Any chance? etc

In the end, it all hung on this. This was a country town. One train a week to all stations south and the City. Two buses, a critical half hour stopover at midnight Tuesdays and Fridays. There was no impassioned good-bye. No good-bye of any kind, really. Just a nod of the head, beaded braids jostle on the denim jacket, and she was gone. I waited, hoping, but there was no rushing realisation in her face, nor a bursting back through the door. She was just gone. The train was gone. Under orange streetlight at the café, for a week, buses doing a quick offload of returning passengers, throwing bags in underneath for outgoing. Her kit wasn't there and she hadn't taken a seat.

It was moments like these when I mulled on a tattoo or becoming an alcoholic. Mused on moving on. But, in the end, it was just another end scene. And definitely, nothing to see here.

PART 3

This is What I Worry About

If there is somehow to be a staying on, a living through, is this contingent on dislocation, disenfranchisement, a knowing of contradiction, clear direction, clues and evidence that no self-respecting citizen detective could ignore, see and pretend they didn't.

This is what my world is. This is what doom-scrolling brings front of mind. Climate change, fire, drought, flood, cyclone and tornado, sea level rise and islands and coastlines covered in rising water. Destruction of habitat of thousands of species representing life on earth, destabilising earth and soil, destruction of forests and bushland. Nuclear war, ordinary old fashioned killing wars, and refugees walking and homeless. Persecution and murder under the name of homophobia, misogyny, trans-hatred. Colonialism, cultural appropriation. Virus in many iterations, rampant.

Peak Alone

Light strengthens. Fox turns from grey to crouching red. Blurred background shapes sharpen as new sun stretches from horizon to dam. Hunting hawk, whistle and trill, alerts dawn watchers to the still presence of Fox at water's-edge reeds. Light is liminal, luminous.

Peak Alone stands cobalt blue against massing grey-lit storm clouds, rain promise tempered by morning sun, expanding light, then fades back into soft grey mist, clouded and hidden by sheeting rain. On every sky-line, burnt forest on peaks and ridges stands out against back lit sky, spindly trunks and branches buzz cut bare. It's all long shutter speed for low light.

sun clouds
straight-line border country
northwards of Eden
in Gulaga's shadow
a respectful remove from Mumbulla
Peak Alone stands off the A1
by country road to Yowrie
by broken fire trail
to a lookout peak requiring resistance to vertigo
seaward views through mist and haze

Map Maker stands enclosed in triangle, surveys,
though cloud obscures sharp outlines of a known world,
searches for horizon landmarks
drunk on sweet heady smell of green good season grass

remembering seasons past Peak Alone waits
to breathe in again, skittering willywillies, waits for another
season of hot air rising, circling, updrafts and thermals,
blowing dust, heat feasting on dryland drought,
parched trees, crispy undergrowth

Yuin, *Fire-Maker*, cool burns, controlled burns, smoke like spirits, blending to mist, fogs sun.

Fox skirts paddock fence, raising feinting plovers outraged at a not-quite-urban intruder, avoids eye contact with alpacas stare and threat, slips through rain, retreats to anonymity in scrubby bushland on mountain foothills. Kookaburras laugh full throated in rain, call rising and falling, echoes dying, silence expectant.

Fox calls, gekkering, warning. We all hear. Slips into dripping undergrowth. A Cinderella who stayed too long.

Our Place

sheep on evening hill side
line dance
their way to night camp

Andromeda's immensity has the propensity to make us feel small. In the night sky, when all is visible, size matters. Connection matters.

cacophony of dogs
alerting
to change in the cosmos

Huddled in five layers of wool, I track the progress of magpie nest building, hesitant to join their conversation. Before the sun has heat in it we hope for a day without our coats. Frost and ice on our boots tell us to be patient and hopeful.

early fog sunrise
still cold—but, see, cows,
planning their day

Taking our galaxy and our place in it at face value one of the few things we can do to keep our feet on the ground, is plant. And gardening companions come in all sizes with many different motivations.

paw prints
on freshly prepared seed bed
make perfect planting holes

Warning to a Fox

This is the story of a tree, old beyond the recall of generations, and an ugly little dry gully, on the sandy edge of town. In black and white, it's an edgy story, but it's also a story where we somehow know the ending before we begin.

That Autumn morning, I fitted my index finger exactly into your paw-print. I imagined I could feel the residual warmth of your living paw where it had broken through the crust of frost, but of course, you were long gone. Gone from my garden, back along the cold tar and away to your den in the reserve.

So, listen, my fox, you are the one for whom this story lives. You are the feral, like me, who should not be here. Our genes are from another time and place, separated from this small country town by oceans in perpetual motion, limitless, high sky and a dreaming of northern constellations, birds returning and leaving, and water, water falling from clouds that are never far on the horizon.

However, we are both here, foreign and making a go of it, doing the best we can.

The sand quarry is where you find the trucks, digger filling the trucks, trucks driving away to the city. The concrete buildings rise and spread, and you would be amazed to see the buildings, a city of cement. Cement is concrete, concrete is sand. That insatiable city is concrete, but first it was sand. And it's our sand, yours and mine.

Every day that you stay in your den in the sand between the roots of the giant river red-gum, the digger is closer, louder, more careless. The river red-gum feels the sand bank loosen, its roots freed, yet grasping for a place to hold.

The dry gully bed waits for the next flash flood, banks broken, rendered useless by the quarry digger in a relentless quest for sand.

And, as the water recedes, the sand is gone. Scoured from the weakened bed and roiling in the one-in-fifty-year boil and surge of storm water.

So, my fox, you should leave now. Move inland. The tree can only die and fall. The river can only foam and rush and spread, flooding the ugly little gully, rolling the fallen tree from channel to channel scouring out the banks, until it catches in the rocks and tangled fencing wire, lies stranded.

Four Tanka

a moment when
the hard slog of physio
transforms to flow
after major surgery
three steps unaided

Santa still sitting
on the tractor, becalmed
in empty paddock
New Year speeds down the highway
how many more days of grace?

on the weekend of Summer Nats
e-scooter burnouts on our rainbow

what use is a dragon fly—
its tiny flameless breath,
faint and muted roar?
feinting and hovering
reed beds sway as it passes

tiny grass wrens
accented in electric blue
wait for us
on the dune grass before
they scatter in the sea wind

Exclusion Zone

Only football can make you feel like this. Like you're at another critical life point, choosing or stumbling into an alternative life path, a 'road not taken' moment. And I'm not holding up football—that inane running up and down of a muddy, sweaty lot of bodies, not trying not to draw blood, chasing a bladder full of air—as a good thing. It's a pointless thing, wasteful. Just as human mobs that defy a pandemic are wastrels. So, when the Ukrainian football team is ranked 25th by FIFA out of 210 teams you've got to wonder, what's the point. That's a nothing, middle of the road, beige on beige ranking.

all life is linked
my gene pool and theirs
by-standing the moment
humans crave crowds and circus
cheering on stupidity

I'm not at a football game, I'm at Western Plains Zoo looking at Przewalski's horse. Under an unreliable eucalyptus shade, in pounding inland summer heat, is the only true wild horse left in the world and the last remaining species of wild horse. Takhi, never domesticated, spirit horse, became extinct in Mongolia's wilderness in 1968, and it is because of zoo based breeding programs that there have been some animals reintroduced back into the wild.

two foals, old gene pool
last remaining wild horses
dreaming spirits
in breathless heat, eucalypt haze
Takhi dream of wolves, snow

The stallion and his mares are grazing, dozing, mud-bathing, and drinking from luke-warm water in a constructed creek. Some are standing nose to tail, dreaming but keeping an eye out, looking out for danger in both directions. Their gene pool knows wolves and undrinkable frozen water in winter. But here, eucalyptus exudes strong blue haze under a sound cloud of cicadas. Visitors are walking past on further paths, looking for big shock jock bang for buck options. Two small foals don't cut it when they could see cheetahs, hippos, Sumatran Tigers … .

In April 1986, plant operators at Chernobyl nuclear power plant in Ukraine make serious mistakes. It's just before the Cold War ends, argy-bargy between international human powers, when things are already starting to unravel. Afterwards, we all ask ourselves, could we have prevented this? Could we have taken another tack on human existence, before we got to this point? In what Universe are we greedy enough to risk humanity? Risk our planet for human excess? Decisions, decisions, decisions. And what we have is the mindlessness of football.

radioactive
Chernobyl habitat
apocalypse
two hundred thousand hectares
towards a post-human planet

We paper over mistakes by spraying radioactive sand with a liquid polymer that hardens to keep it from blowing away. But the barren moonscape is first breached when polymer skin cracks and disintegrates, seeds force their way through. Young pines are planted. Moose, gray wolf, lynx, brown bear, wild horses are handed an opportunity. Humans are excluded.

wild horses and bison
living free in Chernobyl
life on Earth
is all connected
it's on us to get it right

Imagine all those fans at the football, all of them in full throat, just before full time, just seconds on the Doomsday clock. Several stadia worth. And here's why football is important. 207,000 hectares were reduced to apocalyptic devastation. 350,000 Ukrainians were evacuated. The largest sports stadium in the world, in Korea, only holds 114,000 fans, Melbourne Cricket Ground 100,024. What if they were bending their minds to the future of the planet. Rather than cheering on a team where they have no influence on any result. Imagine those people, in scarves and hats, coats, all the football crowds of them, fleeing air they cannot see.

Without over-stepping, we know what happened. We know what happens. A dystopic post-humanity. A short human history.

exclusion zone
humans stay out   rewilding
seeds burst through
polymer covering
let them go on without us

Sestina for Afghanistan

A magpie carols in frigid light as if
sunburst wattle flags a heroic past, when
we all know our invasion history is usually
overlaid with sorry silence. Consistently
we rewrite the past. Whitewash our blame. Perhaps
this brings us to our shameful dereliction now. However,

it will take a lot to expunge our grief and guilt. However
we frame it, detention on an island if
they came by boat, indefinite hell, hope lost. Perhaps
you can imagine children's faces when
told their youth and barbed wire are tied. Consistently
we say that freedom from fear will not usually,

or ever, be granted them. That, usually
detention, uncertainty, visa queues are their lot. However
it is we shout our lucky country pride, consistently
we sink lower still, down to moral failure in Afghanistan. If
desperate pleas that death is certain do not move us, when
we tell thousands of our allies 'it's case by case', perhaps

snail-mail from Kabul gets them through the gate, perhaps
our shame and disgrace at duty failed, this usually
should prompt at least some action. When
guns are fired, mobs screaming, soldiers wait, however, in
whatever tone, we ask 'what are they waiting for?' (as if
tomorrow really is a new dawn) politicians consistently

fail us. Our national government fails us. Consistently
it shirks the test of acting for humanity. Perhaps
if they felt the terror spreading bodily at checkpoints; if
they had ever known persecution of oppressors; usually
this would inspire some empathy. However,
it seems that lacking morals, drunk on power, when

called to act, they think only of themselves. When
I dissent, I say you do not speak for me. Consistently
there is a contradiction in my civil allegiance. However,
I am not alone. Demanding civility not anarchy. Perhaps
this is something too hard for them to understand. Usually,
they could be engaged in discussion, change their minds. If

only this were true. However, history does come out, when
sealed files open. But, read in the future, consistently
we see these crimes re-formed, perhaps whitewashed,
usually …

Black Box

What good is it to me now? A blueprint for post-apocalyptic society. I'm impatient for Apocalypse, however that might show itself, just to get it over with. We have a harbinger, based on coincidence, a perfect storm of two events, both unpleasant but unremarkable in themselves, signalling that we are closer than ever. And a blueprint for After will only be useful if there are survivors. These are stark words but there is no room for the ludic in this polemic, only dire, straight talk, gut punch. To try to open your eyes and ears.

In COVID-empty streets feral pigs are flying, surging, pig bodies growing larger, more and more pig, then enormous. Herds, groups, single foragers bursting unexpectedly and arrogantly out of coastal dune grass and low scrub, numbers increasing, filling town streets and laneways. Spaces we vacated as pandemic rolled in on us from overseas and we retreated to our inner selves, beach houses and suburban isolation; Winnebagos return, queues of them, lumbering, swaying on uncambered narrow bitumen coastal roads, relentless migration of freedom seekers to summer beaches, crowded camping grounds, running wild like dogs in an off-lead area. Pigs and campervans.

After weeks of rain, Peak Alone is just a memory behind low cloud. Unseasonal floods. Unprecedented bushfires. Tornados and cyclones moving south. We've been told its Doomsday for so long now, if Earth crashes as a result of climate change, we can hardly claim surprise. Yes, we could admit to carelessness, greed, avarice, self-centred apathy, of ourselves and our leaders in politics and industry. But we cannot claim no-one told us to change our ways.

Until the Ledger. Until the Black Box. An indestructible recording device powered by sunlight. A data store for at least another fifty years. Record keeping like no other, pure data, inarguable, that will hold leaders to account for our mismanagement and blatant, knowing destruction of wonder, of our blue planet. Locked onto a base of 500-million-year-old granite, it will all be there, laid out for any surviving data nerd or number cruncher to see. How we plundered and wasted the whole living magnificence of life on Earth.

Going for full Mad Max in creating a human wrought apocalypse isn't working out so well for us. If they survive, at Apocalypse apogee, next generations will blame and castigate us. Even as they come out of their bunkers, blink away darkness encrusting their eyes and slowly, dazedly, start their slow search for green.

Don't do what we did. It's an old word *heed*, but prescient. And scarily pertinent. Heed this. We are showing you the pathway to destruction.

Everybody's Off-balance

At the moment, considering drought, bushfires, hailstorms, floods, COVID-19 pandemic, earthquake, everybody's off balance. Although I was just trying to do my job as a human being there were times when I was hormonal. Life is a roller coaster, right? And if being feisty is normal, sometimes it's just seen as rude, although sometimes, seen through a lover's eyes, feisty can be heart-warming.

Ladies, let me go on …

I met her in Nairobi. Intercontinental Hotel. Transit stop. It was an international format. By that I mean it wasn't reality TV or a franchise with public liability insurance. But it was a cosmopolitan style come-on, glances, smiles, hanky dropped, keys left on Dunkin' Donuts counter etc. I could say it was scandalous, but that is a lost word … like travesty, or scurrilous. Although this situation was unusual, I was being the best version of myself, aiming to be real, authentic. Maybe a feminist. But anyway, an assertive woman on her life's journey. Living to the full and so on.

I could segue here to an after story but the analytics are not good. Last night, the last night I decided to call her, call her out. But it was others who were shot, tanked, wasted, pot shotten. And the inheritance, what was left over, what I was left with, was tiny.

So, while I was coming up she was coming down and that just does not do.

Take just one, I thought. No need to be greedy.

—

This is a story of how the immensity of a problem prevents us from imagining anything beyond it. This is a story of uncertainty and desperation of distance. Distance, yet so close her body sweat dampens my T-shirt with tenderness of dew on a wren's nest. Of falling down Alice's rabbit hole. This is a story of dreams and anger. Suppression of queerness is millennial and endemic, collapsing history, straining voices.

I had a dream she said. I was a woman. You know, the dead female body writers need to start their mystery thrillers. I don't know how I died, I just remember knowing that I was the body, the one they needed this time. I wasn't afraid by then, I was angry. That I had to die to start them off. I wondered if being a lesbian was why it had to be me, because that is what trolls say, *Die Bitch … too queer to live!!! All you need is a good fuck!!!* But then I realised it could have been any female body, just as long as our hero could get his rocks off solving why. It's movement from complicated living body to manageable, comprehensible, dead body.

And then she cried, and I held her against my T-shirt, and asked if she wanted a coffee.

—

I am wearied, with reserves exhausted, by things that cannot wait. Food for Afghanistan and education for girls and Taliban mullahs, both of whom need different essential things. Protecting habitats, more than a handful of vital trees, to halt extinction of koalas and Powerful Owls. Ring fencing stands of trees and grasslands to stop plunder and despoilation of grasses and plant species we may have already lost. By girlfriends who need, need, need, who shine their light in my eyes.

It's a numbers game. If we are the purpose of what came before, what a grave responsibility we bear. And how poor and weak our bearing up has been. What little regard we have for our future (if we judge this on our response, what we have not done so far).

School's out and public space is for youth. Roaming, colonising places where only virus has been from beginning to now. Giving life, giving blood and breath. Giving virus. Take up. Take on. Take over. Jostle. Spread. Young women uncomfortable in unfortunate clothes, uneasy eyes. Boys in black, body hugging, spindle shanks, aesthetes slouch, sensitive hands. All voicing loud. Taking space where breath can kill.

—

New year. New resolve. Getting our ducks in a row.

Only at a fun fair are ducks ever in a row. Where pocked and pitted little tin duck cut-outs bumble across a shooting stage, duck their heads as they seem to launch off the end and tip over out of sight. We know they are pinned to a moving wire and will bob up again in range, in a row, waiting for a lucky shot to knock them flat.

In the wild, in whatever's left of wilderness, ducks are rarely ordered, row bound.

Ready for slaughter with unfair, unsporting odds. Massacre, blood need, bloodletting.

Should our appointed leaders have had our game plan be more than a plan before letting Omicron rage unchecked? Not enough Rapid Antigen Tests. All rules relaxed. Duty of care, too little, too late. Leaving us sitting ducks. Crouched in fragile reeds, nests of tussock bent. Ducking for cover, avoiding joining breath, staying put and masking up.

Inlet waters rise, foot by foot, over the end of the bed. Over our feet. Too late now for ducks in a row …

—

I was always trying to make sense of it. Make my sense of it. Our relationship was like a shift in available light. Like running after sunlight. The moon figures in it all, with hormonal tides running strongly with mood, against mood. So anything untoward has a built-in alibi. When I look back, a messy, devastating ending took about a year. She never said she was finished with it, with me. Not to me. Only to her friends. Who then asked me about it, about her? And when I asked her, incoherently and in a somewhat (in retrospect) immoderate way, she said yes, it was obvious wasn't it?

But here's what it was. She kept ringing me, emailing, when she was upset, lonely, needed a problem talking through, wanted reassurance about something, felt overwhelmed by her fab job at a fancy school in Hong Kong. So, to me it wasn't at all clear. My ducks were all over the place, far from any row.

And through all this, I heard later, through the same friends, that her ex-husband thought she was off thinking things (him) through, and would come back to him, them.

So, I was never clear. Was she lying? To me? To herself? And if so, what about, specifically?

Now, looking back, *liar, cheat, user*, are words that still have a cathartic effect. Forgiveness, perspective, distance, rarely figure in the equation. I keep looking for reasons for schadenfreude. Moving on, but with the satisfaction of baggage.

—

When we woke the rainstorm had gone. Runnels busily drained themselves into small rough channels presaging beginnings of erosion. Sky was again itself without dark overdressing. Downpipes had divested themselves of their excessively thunderous rattle and settled into their usual silent verticals. Ducks winged in mobs from one side of the window to the other. The dog sighed from under blanket rumple and settled firmly into stay-here-longer mode.

I could see the *liar cheat user* on the other side of the bed, her eyes open, assuming her luminous saintly aureole as waking took hold and moved to the irreversible. Today she is the other, her luminosity is righteous, nearly perfect, colour muted and hued and glowing. Perfection unassailable.

Starting the day wrong-footed, uncoloured, as usual, I wonder if my aura will move out of the brown, beige, unpromising colour palette and into something more attractive. I'll make the tea I said. Elusive light, after an incandescent rage of betrayal subsides. What's left is not so much a clean sharp black but a slow, ponderous grey or even a brown. A no-colour that can't get up energy to run, moves with resigned deliberation.

—

I've survived my life until this point in time is reached, when singing and dancing are banned. Auras are allowed if not dependent on exchange of air, a breath of air is air too much. Also, colours are allowed if within the colour chart canon so they can be interpreted to best advantage. An aureole can be a good sign. Although I feel I am not congenitally required to sing and dance, seeing others, seeing her, move and sway and rock and roll is interesting to me, even though it makes me feel breathless and a bit off balance. When she mourns the world of song and movement, it takes light and balance from my world too.

PART 4

How Does it End?

Getting past the wifecarrying/wifetossing/shootingwifeoutofcannon local agricultural annual show spectacular, I'm just kicking the story on. Not giving a free pass to hate speech, not letting a religious protection ooze beyond its borders into an anti-gay weapon. It's an error catastrophe, a high risk, wishful hopeful …

IT'S A JOURNEY

How does it end, these last days, this journey through a queer forest of three hundred thousand years, humans peopling the world? Undergrowth, overgrowth, overstory … do they tell a story? Stale sharp reek of fecundity, too much of too much avid green, vivid lost forest we've lived in. Growing garden, growing crop, cropping dust rising, soil lost, wind-blown, storm blown, vital volcanic, friable, only viable vis-à-vis organic matter, grass, roots, weeds, rooted, rotted, decomposed residue residing in mineral soil. Leaves, branches, bark, stems, soft groundcover.

Fire, burn out, burnt out, burn over and slow burn, cool burn of forest floor and top story. Our will to move, peripatetic, is some man going somewhere. Spreading out, populating horizons. Not settled, not staying put.

Rain bomb, flash flood, flashing flood, washing out, eroding gullies or slow relentless rising river. Seep water finds its own level, untrammelled, unconstrained, uncontrolled green.

Natural selection of favoured genes after this pandemic. It doesn't end, we just stop caring that someday, somehow, it *will* end, when enough humans are not found. Pandemics always end.

When we come back to the world as we know it, as we left it, storms, extinctions, disasters, blue planet cannot host us. Benign is gone, liveable gone, survivable gone.

When our species dies, how does it end?

Moving On

The climate we were born in no longer exists—our heating planet reasserts itself after humanity's destruction. Particle clouds shift revealing our blue planet post-human existence—we watch safely from an expat galaxy. After all this, we still have a fascination with evil.

The new science solves identikit problems when villains' masks reveal only eyes—balaclavas are obsolete on this new world. Everybody continues an homage to our last days on Earth, wearing K95s, N95s, P2s as a fashion statement for the new world, but built for the dozen plus one of us from a 3D printer housed in the techno unit nestled safely in the cramped nosecone of our evacuation rocket.

I can hear the voices of the dead from here, asking *why are you on The List for escape?* and *can escape be read as a salvation of sorts?*

I find I cannot answer them, these voices of the dead, those left behind. Right place at right time seems a bit glib. But I was inside the hatch, welding a mini bar into place, overseen by a pretty useless zoom monitor (I mean, we were all in the ship, no-one to zoom at/to/with).

It happened like this. When the time came they bundled in, all twelve of those on The List, pushing me towards the back, hatch oiled its way closed with a hiss and soft thwuck suction seal. We were off and running, so to speak before anyone even saw me to ask *what the hell are you doing here? You aren't on The List.*

Having failed to become what I might have been, nothing has cost me more than that day. Disconnected from anything urgent, I have become a recorder of the actions of others. Manqué human. Like the rest of humanity. Not living up to our designated humanist-liberal potential.

Hello Trojan

At the same time as the torch in the Chinese Torch Relay for the Winter Olympics Beijing 2022 was carried by underwater robots in Lake Yongding, we were captivated by our awareness of a Trojan Asteroid, travelling ahead of us, in our trajectory around the sun.

Given this particular Trojan will be Earth's companion for the next 4,000 years, the first thing we asked of it is *Can we visit?* Or *We could do a fly-by, no breath exchanged, just to say hello, we know you are there, are you ok?* Just hoping it isn't keeping different hours from us, and we won't be too unwelcome. Hoping our reputation for planetary destruction hasn't preceded us.

So, kicking the story on, down a one-street main-street, aggression in a hawking spit, into a cool green hippy-dippy, gay-embracing, latte-loving, over-thinking, elitist bookshop, finding words for safety, sanctuary, protection …

For politicians we give the gift of war. So they can spin and spin and gas-light and jostle and betray and kill for power. For ourselves we claim the tactics of regret and separation. We see that the island is closed, sigh and look outwards. Look to a place where the churches and mosques are still standing. Are they roofless? Look out into the channel where whales and dolphins live shy and circumspectly. Is the reef so white it's dead? Resurrectable?

We take hubris from uncertain and moving ground, desperate departures, dread. And we regret the crimes of aggression and procrastination and inertia and self-obsession and anthropo-selfishness.

The poets keep writing, into the mouth of the end of the world, up until the moment of nuclear or carbon emissions extinction.
Why do we keep writing if the world is ending?
We do it because …
Because, what if it doesn't?

It Becomes Her

sometimes a dream becomes a woman
and what becomes her

in the becoming, a dream is to the woman
what the ocean is to skin, and that becomes her

lying on her board, waiting for a wave,
rocking with any swell the ocean sends her

woman becomes the ocean
and the waves become her

whatever dream becomes the ocean
the woman is the ocean and it becomes her

She Goes to Town
by Sandra Renew

This book was written on Ngunnawal and Ngambri land (Canberra) and Yuin land (Cobargo).

First published 2024

POETRY
© 2024 Sandra Renew
ISBN: 978-0-6459209-8-7

All rights reserved. No part of this book may be reproduced without permission of the author or publisher, except for brief quotes for review purposes.

BOOK, TYPSETTING, AND LOGO DESIGN
Mountains Brown Press

PUBLISHER
Life Before Man
Gazebo Books
PO Box 375
Summer Hill
New South Wales 2130
Australia

gazebobooks.com.au

2 4 6 8 10 9 7 5 3 1

This book was made possible thanks to Anthony Mark Day